Mountains

by Kimberly M. Hutmacher

Consulting Editor: Gail Saunders-Smith, PhD

Consultant: Nikki Strong, PhD
St. Anthony Falls Laboratory
University of Minnesota

CAPSTONE PRESS
a capstone imprint

Pebble Plus is published by Capstone Press,
151 Good Counsel Drive, P.O. Box 669, Mankato, Minnesota 56002.
www.capstonepub.com

032010
005740CGF10

Books published by Capstone Press are manufactured with paper
containing at least 10 percent post-consumer waste.

Library of Congress Cataloging-in-Publication Data
Hutmacher, Kimberly.
    Mountains / by Kimberly M. Hutmacher.
    p. cm.—(Pebble plus. Natural wonders)
    Includes bibliographical references and index.
    Summary: "Simple text and full-color photos explain how mountains form and why they are an important
landform"—Provided by publisher.
    ISBN 978-1-4296-5004-5 (library binding)
    ISBN 978-1-4296-5590-3 (paperback)
    1. Mountains—Juvenile literature. I. Title. II. Series.
GB512.H88 2011
551.43'2—dc22   2010002792

Editorial Credits
Katy Kudela, editor; Heidi Thompson, designer; Kelly Garvin, media researcher; Eric Manske, production specialist

Photo Credits
Dreamstime/David Watts Jr., 17; Henrik Andersen, 5; Jason Cheever, 9; Mike Norton, cover; Oleksandr Burtovyy, 7;
    Robflint, 11
Fotolia/Alexey Stiop, 13
Shutterstock/amachado, 21; Jason Maehl, 15; Pichugin Dmitry, 1
Super Stock Inc./Newberry Library, 19

Note to Parents and Teachers

The Natural Wonders series supports national geography standards related to the physical and
human characteristics of places. This book describes and illustrates mountains. The images
support early readers in understanding the text. The repetition of words and phrases helps early
readers learn new words. This book also introduces early readers to subject-specific vocabulary
words, which are defined in the Glossary section. Early readers may need assistance to read
some words and to use the Table of Contents, Glossary, Read More, Internet Sites, and Index
sections of the book.

Table of Contents

How a Mountain Forms

Under Earth's surface, plates

pull apart and push together.

Over time, pieces of crust

push to the surface.

There, mountains stand tall.

Mountains form
when two plates
smash together.
The plates crumple and
fold up into a mountain.

How Plates
Form Mountains

Plate 2

Plate 1

7

Other forces form mountains.

On Earth's surface, glaciers

slowly move across the land.

These ice masses carve out

mountains and valleys.

From underground, melted
rock rises to Earth's surface.
The melted rock hardens and
shapes volcanoes on the land.
Volcanoes are mountains too.

Famous Mountains

Mountains often stand
together in a group.
The Andes Mountain range
stretches along the coast
of South America.

Mount Everest is the world's tallest mountain. Part of the Himalaya range, it stands 29,035 feet (8,850 meters) tall.

In the United States, the
Rocky Mountains stretch
from New Mexico to Alaska.
People visit these mountains
to camp and hike.

People and Mountains

Long ago, mountain travel

took planning.

People had to find

their own paths through

the steep slopes.

Today travel is much easier.

Roads zigzag

across mountains.

People even build towns

in mountain ranges.

Glossary

coast—the place where the land and the ocean meet

crust—the hard outer layer of Earth

glacier—a large mass or sheet of ice found in high mountains or polar areas

Himalaya—a mountain range in Asia; it is the highest mountain range in the world

plate—large pieces of Earth's crust that fit together like pieces of a jigsaw puzzle

range—a long chain of mountains

valley—an area of low ground between two hills or mountains; rivers and lakes often form in valleys

volcano—a mountain with vents through which molten lava, ash, cinders, and gas erupt

Read More

Green, Emily K. *Mountains*. Learning About the Earth. Minneapolis: Bellwether Media, 2007.

Mis, Melody S. *Exploring Mountains*. Geography Zone: Landforms. New York: PowerKids Press, 2009.

Internet Sites

FactHound offers a safe, fun way to find Internet sites related to this book. All of the sites on FactHound have been researched by our staff.

Here's all you do:

Visit www.facthound.com

FactHound will fetch the best sites for you!

Index

Word Count: 172
Grade: 1
Early-Intervention Level: 24